MW00949237

COMMUNITY HELPERS

Welders

by Betsy Rathburn

BLASTOFF! READERS

BELLWETHER MEDIA • MINNEAPOLIS, MN

Note to Librarians, Teachers, and Parents:

Blastoff! Readers are carefully developed by literacy experts and combine standards-based content with developmentally appropriate text.

Level 1 provides the most support through repetition of high-frequency words, light text, predictable sentence patterns, and strong visual support.

Level 2 offers early readers a bit more challenge through varied simple sentences, increased text load, and less repetition of high-frequency words.

Level 3 advances early-fluent readers toward fluency through increased text and concept load, less reliance on visuals, longer sentences, and more literary language.

Level 4 builds reading stamina by providing more text per page, increased use of punctuation, greater variation in sentence patterns, and increasingly challenging vocabulary.

Level 5 encourages children to move from "learning to read" to "reading to learn" by providing even more text, varied writing styles, and less familiar topics.

Whichever book is right for your reader, Blastoff! Readers are the perfect books to build confidence and encourage a love of reading that will last a lifetime!

This edition first published in 2020 by Bellwether Media, Inc.

No part of this publication may be reproduced in whole or in part without written permission of the publisher. For information regarding permission, write to Bellwether Media, Inc., Attention: Permissions Department, 6012 Blue Circle Drive, Minnetonka, MN 55343.

Library of Congress Cataloging-in-Publication Data

LC record for Welders available at https://lccn.loc.gov/2019024897

Text copyright © 2020 by Bellwether Media, Inc. BLASTOFF! READERS and associated logos are trademarks and/or registered trademarks of Bellwether Media, Inc.

Editor: Kate Moening   Designer: Brittany McIntosh

Printed in the United States of America, North Mankato, MN.

Table of Contents

Melting Metal

A welder fixes a broken car part. She carefully places the **metal** pieces.

She flips down her mask. She lights her **torch**. Time to make **sparks** fly!

sparks

7

What Are Welders?

Welders work with metal. Some make cars or buildings. Others work on roads or bridges!

These helpers often work on **construction sites**. They also **weld** in special **workshops**.

workshop

What Do Welders Do?

Welders cut, shape, and join metal. They read plans to see how parts fit together.

plans

Welder Gear

welding mask   gloves   torch   earplugs

13

These helpers
fix machines.
They use torches
to join broken
metal pieces.

torch

15

Welders follow
safety rules.
Masks and
gloves help
keep them safe!

What Makes a Good Welder?

Welders are careful. Their work sites can be full of danger!

Welders follow plans and weld neat lines. They help build the world!

Glossary

construction sites

places where workers build buildings

torch

a long tool welders use that makes fire; torches weld metal together.

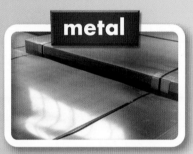

metal

a material that is usually shiny and hard

weld

to join pieces of metal by heating the edges until they melt together

sparks

small pieces of burning material that come from a fire

workshops

places where things are made or fixed

To Learn More

AT THE LIBRARY
Bowman, Chris. *Construction Workers*. Minneapolis,
Minn.: Bellwether Media, 2018.

Leaf, Christina. *Mechanics*. Minneapolis, Minn.:
Bellwether Media, 2019.

Waxman, Laura Hamilton. *Construction Worker
Tools*. Minneapolis, Minn.: Lerner Publications, 2020.

ON THE WEB

FACTSURFER

Factsurfer.com gives you
a safe, fun way to find
more information.

1. Go to www.factsurfer.com.

2. Enter "welders" into the search box and click 🔍.

3. Select your book cover to see a list of related
   web sites.

Index

The images in this book are reproduced through the courtesy of: Tawansak, front cover, pp. 14-15; DuxX, pp. 4-5, 6-7; Bannafarsai_Stock, pp. 8-9; Kumpol Vashiraaskorn, pp. 10-11; GrapeImages, pp. 12-13; tale, p. 13 (welding mask); AlexTois, p. 13 (gloves); lertkaleepic, p. 13 (torch); photo one, p. 13 (earplugs); SasinTipchai, pp. 16-17; King Ropes Access, pp. 18-19; shinobi, pp. 20-21; Perfect Gui, p. 22 (construction sites); quka, p. 22 (metal); Volodymyr Burdiak, p. 22 (sparks); svetlovskiy, p. 22 (torch); Praphan Jampala, p. 22 (weld); Halfpoint, p. 22 (workshops).